Lupita
MA 992.

25475
4 7543

Survival
Spanish

Survival
Spanish

by Diethard Lübke
illustrated by Theo Scherling

LANGENSCHEIDT PUBLISHERS
New York, Berlin, Munich, Vienna, Zurich

Publisher: Langenscheidt Publishers, Inc.
Managing Editor: Jessie G. McGuire
U.S. Editorial Direction: Anne & Jean Wadier
U.S. Adaptation: Cory Reed
Cover Design: Vera Benson
Production: Ripinsky & Company
Letters: We welcome your comments and suggestions.
                          Our address: Langenscheidt Publishers, Inc.
                          46-35 54th Road
                          Maspeth, NY 11378

Important Reader Information

We have not burdened you with special grammatical rules. Phonetic transcriptions have been simplified as much as possible and are found in the grey boxes next to the English/ Spanish word list in each chapter.

This will also help you to fill in the cartoon balloons with Spanish phrases. Each blank line stands for one letter. For an example, refer to page 10.

To make things easier for you, English sentence structure has been adjusted to the Spanish phrases. Therefore, English sentences may sound somewhat clumsy at times.

Throughout the book, only the latest facts are given, as of 1990. They were carefully checked by the author and the publisher. However, we are not responsible for any changes that may have occurred.

Translated, adapted and revised from *Spanisch—Jetzt in Comics,*
© 1988 by Humboldt-Taschenbuchverlag Jacobi KG, München.

Manufactured in the United States of America

ISBN: 0-88729-258-5

Contents

¡Hola, señora! ¡Hola, señor! 7

1 Airport 8

2 Car 12

3 Hotel 16

4 Breakfast 20

5 Museum 24

6 A coffee 30

7 Exchange 34

8 Postcards 40

9 At the Beach 44

10 Fruit 50

11 Reservations 54

12 At the Restaurant 58

13 Drinks 64

14 Sick 68

15 Taxi 72

Answers 77

Food and Drink 89

Mini-Dictionary for Tourists 91

Numbers 100

Syllable Puzzle 106

Word-Building Puzzle 108

Important Addresses 110

¡Hola, señora!
¡Hola, señor!

We are pleased that you want to start learning Spanish and intend to travel to a Spanish-speaking country. Many tourists visit Spain and Latin America every year because they love **el sol, el vino, la playa** and much more. Knowing a little Spanish will help you understand and be understood in typical situations—and your attempts to speak Spanish will be appreciated by everyone you encounter.

This entertaining and informative approach to the language does not require you to "cram" vocabulary and "slave over" grammar, as in school. It does not prepare you for a test, but rather is simply meant to afford you greater pleasure on your vacation, without requiring much effort. Make yourself comfortable, pick up a pencil. You will see that learning Spanish can be very enjoyable.

In order to help your communication skills in a variety of Spanish-speaking countries, this book uses standard vocabulary easily recognized in both Latin America and Spain. Pronunciation conforms to Spanish of the Americas.

So you can get right into the swing of things, we have prepared cartoon balloons for you to fill in. Each blank stands for one letter. And now we will introduce a few important words. The pronunciation is in square brackets:

Buenos días	[boo•e′nōs dē′äs]	*Good morning/day (before lunch)*
Buenas tardes	[boo•e′näs tär′des]	*Good afternoon/ evening (after lunch)*
Buenas noches	[boo•e′näs nō′tshes]	*Good evening/night (after dark)*
Hola	[ō′lä]	*Hello*
Adiós	[ädyōs′]	*Goodbye*
Gracias	[grä′syäs]	*Thank you*
Sí	[sē]	*Yes*
No	[nō]	*No*

ävyōn'	el avión	*airplane*
voo•e'lō	el vuelo	*flight*
voo•e'lō dyesēse'ēs	el vuelo dieciséis	*flight 16*
de dōn'de	¿De dónde	*Where does . . . [it]*
sä'le	sale . . . ?	*leave from?*
poo•er'tä	la puerta	*gate*
noo'merō dōs	número dos	*number two*
kye'rō	quiero . . .	*I'd like . . .*
fäktoorär'	facturar	*to check (luggage)*
mäle'tä	la maleta	*suitcase*
ekēpä'he	el equipaje	*luggage*
pōr fävōr'	por favor	*please*
grä'syäs	gracias	*thank you*
tärhe'tä de embär'ke	la tarjeta de embarque	*boarding pass*
soo	su	*your*
moo'ē byen	muy bien	*very well*
senyōr'	señor	*sir*

1 Airport

NOTE: Answers for the dialogues in each chapter can be found starting on page 77.

bōle'tō	el boleto	*ticket*
tō'me soo bōle'tō	tome su boleto	*take your ticket*
se'dä el pä'sō*	ceda el paso	*yield*
gäsōlē'nä	la gasolina	*gasoline*
gäsōlē'nä soo'per	gasolina super	*super gasoline*
koo•än'tō	¿cuánto?	*How much?*
lye'nō	lleno	*full*
lye'nō pōr fävōr'	lleno, por favor	*fill it, please*
pe'sō	el peso	*peso (Mexico)*
mēl pe'sōs	mil pesos	*1000 pesos*
dyes mēl pe'sōs	diez mil pesos	*10,000 pesos*
pe se'tä	la peseta	*peseta (Spain)*
pōr fävōr'	por favor	*please*

Tolls and Travel

On many major Spanish and Latin American highways a toll (**peaje**) may be collected. Remember that the metric system is used in Spain and most of Latin America. 10 kilometers = approximately 6 miles; one gallon = 3.8 liters (one liter is approximately 2 pints).

Gender of Nouns

In Spanish all nouns reflect one of two genders; masculine: using the article **el** (plural: **los**), and feminine: **la** (plural: **las**).

Plural

In Spanish, the plural ends in "s": **el peso/los pesos; la peseta/las pesetas**

---

* In Spain the [s] sound of the letter "c" (as in "ceda el paso") and the letter "z" is pronounced [ø], similar to the English [th] sound in "thing" or "thank you."

2 Car

14

YIELD →

__ _____, ___ _____.
Your ticket, please.

___ _____.
1000 pesos.

OAXACA 10

Organize a trip from Puerto Vallarta to Oaxaca. You may wish to consult a road map or atlas.

Puerto Vallarta | México | Cuernavaca
Guadalajara | Puebla | Morelia | Oaxaca

_____ , _____ , _____ , _____ ,
_____ , _____ , _____ .

äbētäsyōn'	la habitación	room
oo'nä äbētäsyōn' dō'ble	una habitación doble	double room
pre'syō	el precio	price
koo•än'tō koo•es'tä la äbētäsyōn'	¿Cuánto cuesta la habitación?	How much is the room?
la tō'mō	la tomo	I'll take it
dē'ä	el día	day
pärä koo•än'tōs dē'äs	¿para cuántos días?	For how many days?
pä'rä sēng'kō dē'äs	para cinco días	for five days
boo•e'näs tär'des	buenas tardes	good afternoon
senyōr'	señor	sir, Mr.
senyō'rä	señora	madam, Mrs.
sē	sí	yes
moo'ē byen	muy bien	very well

Hotel Categories

Hotels are classified in categories which range from 5-star hotels to a simple **residencia**. The price list (**precios globales** = all-inclusive prices) are posted at the reception desk and in the rooms. In Spain, **paradores** were once old palaces, castles or monasteries, and are now state-owned hotels. They are often situated in particularly beautiful locations and are classified as good or very good hotels.

This, these

The demonstrative pronouns are: masculine = **este** (plural: **estos**), feminine = **esta** (plural: **estas**).

Adjectives

The endings of adjectives must agree with the gender of the modified noun. In general, the endings are: masculine = **o** (plural: **os**), feminine = **a** (plural: **as**). Example: **bueno, buenos / buena, buenas.**

* The balloons at the beginning of each lesson are illustrations only and do not require you to translate them.

3 Hotel

18

¿---- ------- ----?
For how many days?

---- ----- ----.
For five days.

¿------- ------ -- --------?
How much is the room?

----- --- --------.
5000 pesetas.

--- ----.
Very well.

-- ----.
I'll take it.

→
1 Price
3 Day
5 Room
6 Mr.

↓
2 Five
4 Well

19

boo•e'nōs dē'äs	**buenos días**	*good day/morning*
kōmedōr'	**el comedor**	*dining room*
käfe' kōn le'tshe	**café con leche**	*coffee with milk*
te	**el té**	*tea*
pänesē'lyō	**el panecillo**	*roll*
mermelä'dä	**la mermelada**	*jam*
mäntekē'lyä	**la mantequilla**	*butter*
hoo'gō	**el jugo**	*juice*
hoo'gō de närän'hä	**jugo de naranja**	*orange juice*
dese'ä ooste'	**¿Desea usted . . . ?**	*Would you like . . . ?*
dōn'de estä'	**¿Dónde está . . . ?**	*Where is . . . ?*
äkē' tye'ne ooste'	**Aquí tiene Ud. . . .**	*Here you have . . .*
ä lä dere'tshä	**a la derecha**	*to/on the right*
ō	**o**	*or*
ē	**y**	*and*

Breakfast

Breakfast in Latin America and Spain is not as large as in the U.S. It usually consists of coffee, tea or hot chocolate, some sort of bread or pastry, and perhaps butter and jam.

"j"

In Spanish, the letter "j" is pronounced [h], as in "hot", only harsher and more guttural.

Ud.

Ud. is the abbreviation for **usted** ("you", polite form). It is sometimes also abbreviated **Vd.**

Es / está

I am = **soy/estoy**; he is = **es/está**; they are = **son/están**. The forms **soy, es, son** designate permanent properties and determinations of time. The forms **estoy, está, están** designate transitory properties and determinations of location.

4 Breakfast

____ _____ __. __ ____,
Here you have the coffee,

__ _____,

__ _____,
the roll, the jam,

_ __ _____.
and the butter.

¿_____ __. ____ __ _____?
Would you like orange juice?

__.
Yes.

→
2 Butter
4 Roll
5 Jam

↓
1 Milk
3 Tea

In the morning,
a visit to the Prado.
In the afternoon . . .

ōfēsē'nä de toorēs'mō	la oficina de turismo	*tourist office*
gē'ä	el guía	*guide (person)*
gē'ä	la guía	*guidebook*
oo'nä gē'ä de mädrēd'	una guía de Madrid	*a guide to Madrid*
moose'ō	el museo	*museum*
moose'ō del prä'dō	el Museo del Prado	*The Prado Museum*
enträ'dä	la entrada	1. *admission ticket* 2. *entrance*
päse'ō	el paseo	*avenue/mall*
en el päse'ō del prä'dō	en el Paseo del Prado	*on Prado Avenue*
outōboos'	el autobús	*bus*
es'te outōboos' vä al moose'ō	este autobús va al museo	*This bus goes to the museum*
nō	no	1. *no* 2. *not*
nō se	no sé	*I don't know*
moo'tshäs grä'syäs	muchas gracias	*thank you very much*
de nä'dä	de nada	*you're welcome*

Museums

Many museums in Spain are only open in the morning and late afternoon and are closed on Monday and Sunday afternoons. The Prado (**Museo del Prado**) in Madrid is one of the world's major museums. It houses paintings by Rafael, Titian, El Greco, Velázquez, Rubens, Goya, Bosch and many others.

5 Museum

____ ___. __ _____.
Take the bus.

¿__ ____ _____
Does this bus go

__ _____ ___ _____?
to the Prado Museum?

___.
Yes.

5 Museum

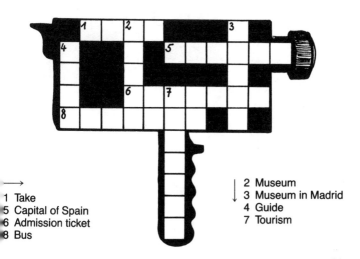

→
1 Take
5 Capital of Spain
6 Admission ticket
8 Bus

↓ 2 Museum
3 Museum in Madrid
4 Guide
7 Tourism

käfe' sō'lō	el café solo	black coffee
vē'nō	el vino	wine
sēgärrē'lyō	el cigarrillo	cigarette
kälōr'	el calor	heat
ke kälōr' ä'se	¡qué calor hace!	How hot it is! (weather)
sōl	el sol	sun
espä'nyä	España	Spain
me'hēkō	México	Mexico
estä'dōs oonē'dōs	Estados Unidos	United States
känädä'	Canadá	Canada
nōrte•ämērekä'nō	norteamericano	American (man)
nōrte•ämērekä'nä	norteamericana	American (woman)
känädyen'se	canadiense	Canadian
es ooste'	¿es Ud.	Are you American?
nōrte•ämērēkänō	norteamericano?	
soi de nooe'vä yōrk	soy de Nueva York	I'm from New York.
me encän'tä	me encanta	I really like (love)
bonē'tō, bōnē'tä	bonito, bonita	pretty, beautiful
tämbyen'	también	also, too

Coffee

Café solo is usually served in small cups; café con leche is served in standard-sized or larger cups with a generous amount of hot milk. Sometimes black coffee or espresso is also called espreso.

Tobacco

Cigarettes may be found in a variety of local tobacco shops, usually plainly labeled by the sign tabaco or tabacalera. In some locations, pipe tobacco may be more difficult to find.

---

* "Maja nude" is a famous painting by Goya (1746–1828).

6 A coffee

änteō'hōs de sōl	anteojos de sol	*sunglasses*
kooän'tō kooes'tän lōs änteō'hōs de sōl	¿cuánto cuestan los anteojos de sol?	*How much are the sunglasses?*
lōs tō'mō	los tomo	*I'll take them*
bōl'sä	la bolsa	*bag*
äl'gō mäs	¿algo más?	*Something else?*
ai	hay	*there is, there are*
oon (oo'nä)	un (una)	*a, an*
bäng'kō	el banco	*bank*
ōfēsē'nä de käm'byō	oficina de cambio	*exchange office*
kämbyär'	cambiar	*to exchange*
kye'rō kämbyär'	quiero cambiar	*I'd like to exchange*
dō'lär	el dólar	*dollar*
dōsyen'tōs dō'läres	doscientos dólares	*200 dollars*
koo•ätrōsyen'tōs mēl	cuatrocientos mil	*400,000*
sōn koo•ätrōsyen'tōs mēl pe'sōs	son cuatrocientos mil pesos	*that's 400,000 pesos*
a•ē'	ahí	*over there*
adyōs'	adiós	*goodbye*

Anteojos de sol

In Spain, the word **gafas** is used instead of **anteojos**; in some parts of Latin America, **lentes** is also used.

Doscientos, trescientos . . .

The endings for the numbers 200 and up vary according to the gender of the noun: **doscientos dólares** (*dólar* is masculine); **doscientas pesetas** (*peseta* is feminine).

Written numbers

In Spanish, the use of commas and decimal points with numbers is opposite of their use in English. For example **400,000 pesos** in Spanish would be written **400.000 pesos**.

7 Exchange

37

7 Exchange

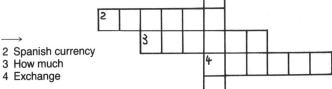

→
2 Spanish currency
3 How much
4 Exchange

↓ 1 Bank

pōstäl′	**la postal**	*postcard*
e′stäs pōstä′les	**estas postales**	*these postcards*
koo•än′tō koo•es′tä	**¿cuánto cuesta**	*How much is a*
oo′nä pōstäl	**una postal?**	*postcard?*
tēm′bre	**el timbre**	*postage stamp*
tye′ne ooste′	**¿tiene Ud.**	*Do you have*
tēm′bres	**timbres?**	*stamps?*
pä′rä estä′dōs	**para Estados**	*to the U.S.*
oonē′dōs	**Unidos**	
ōfēsē′nä de	**la oficina de**	*post office*
corre′os	**correos**	
tresyen′tōs	**trescientos**	*three hundred*
syen	**cien**	*one hundred*
sēng′kō tēm′bres de	**cinco timbres de**	*five 100-peso stamps*
syen pesōs	**cien pesos**	

Post Offices
Post Offices are usually open from 9:00 AM to 1:30 PM and from 4:00 PM to 7:00 PM.

Stamps
In Mexico, postage stamps are called **timbres** (tēm′bres) and in Spain they are called **sellos** (se′lyōs). Small quantities of stamps can also be purchased in the tobacco stores, called **estancos**, recognizable by the sign **tabaco** or **tabacalera**.

Mailboxes
Look for mailboxes marked **extranjero** (foreign countries). When mailing postcards to the U.S. or abroad, be sure to specify **por avión** (air mail) to avoid delays.

8 Postcards

1 Postcard
2 Stamps (Spain)
3 Post office
4 Two hundred

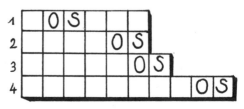

9 At the Beach
En la playa

plä'yä	la playa	beach
pätēn'	el patín	paddle boat
sōmbrē'lyä	la sombrilla	beach umbrella
dōs mēl	dos mil	two thousand
äse'ēte	el aceite	suntan oil
brōnse•ädōr'	bronceador	
elä'dō	el helado	ice cream
vinē'lyä	vainilla	vanilla
tshōkōlä'te	chocolate	chocolate
fre'sä	fresa	strawberry
ō'rä	la hora	hour
pōr ō'rä	por hora	per hour
kä'rō	caro	expensive
moo'ē kä'rō	muy caro	very expensive

Beaches

Beaches in Spain and most in Latin America are public and no entrance fee is charged.

9 At the Beach

__ _____.
A paddle boat.

¿_____ _____
How much is it

___ ____?
per hour?

___ ___ _____.
2000 pesos.

__ ___ ____.
It's very expensive.

47

9 At the Beach

→
3 Ice cream
5 Oil
7 Beach umbrella
8 Hour

↓ 1 Chocolate
2 Vanilla
4 Strawberry
6 Expensive

froo'tä	la fruta	*fruit*
legoom'bres	legumbres	*vegetables*
närän'hä	la naranja	*orange*
plä'tänō	el plátano	*banana*
lōs plä'tänōs estän'	los plátanos están	*The bananas are*
moo'ē boo•e'nōs	muy buenos	*very good*
tōmä'te	el tomate	*tomato*
letshoo'gä	la lechuga	*lettuce*
oon kē'lō de	un kilo de	*a kilo of tomatoes*
tōmä'tes	tomates	
pä'rä	para	*for*
ensälä'dä de	ensalada de	*tomato salad*
tōmä'tes	tomates	
ä'hō	el ajo	*garlic*
oo'nä käbe'sä de	una cabeza de	*a head of garlic*
ä'hōs	ajos	
mēre ooste' lōs	mire Ud. los	*Look at the garlic.*
ä'hōs	ajos	
ke kye're ooste'	¿qué quiere Ud.?	*What would you like?*
sē	sí!	*Yes!*

¡Buen provecho!

To wish an enjoyable meal to others who are eating, the expressions **¡Buen provecho!** and **¡Que aproveche!** are used. These are roughly the equivalent of the French "Bon Appetit."

Weights and measures

In Mexico and Spain, the metric system is used. One kilogram (**kilo**) is approximately 2.2 U.S. pounds (**libras**), and one liter (**litro**) is the equivalent of about 1 U.S. quart (**cuarto de galón**). In Puerto Rico, the U.S. system is used.

10 Fruit

¿___ _____ __.?
What would you like?

_____ _____.
5 oranges.

¿____ ___?
Something else?

__ ____ __ _____,
A kilo of tomatoes,

___ _____.
please.

___ _____ _____
The bananas are
___ _____.
very good.

__, _____.
No, thank you.

____ __, ___ ____.
Look at the garlic.

¡--, --!
No, no!

--!
Yes!

___ _____ __ ____.
A head of garlic.

__ ___ __ ___ _____ ____
Garlic is very good for

_____ __ _____. _-
tomato salad.

1

2

3

4

dē'gäme	**dígame**	*hello (on the telephone)**
reservär'	**reservar**	*to reserve*
me'sä	**la mesa**	*table*
persō'nä	**la persona**	*person*
dōs persō'näs	**dos personas**	*two people*
nōm'bre	**el nombre**	*name*
soo nōm'bre	**su nombre**	*your name*
mē nōm'bre	**mi nombre**	*my name*
äpelyē'dō	**el apellido**	*last name*
mänyä'nä	**mañana**	*tomorrow*
äs'tä mänyä'nä	**hasta mañana**	*until tomorrow*
nō'tshe	**la noche**	*night*
mänyä'nä pōr lä nō'tshe	**mañana por la noche**	*tomorrow night*

Calling home

It is more convenient to place long distance calls at the central telephone office (**oficina de teléfonos**—Mexico; **le telefónica**—Spain), as many hotels make sizeable surcharges for use of the phone. Additionally, most telephone offices offer a special booth (**cabina**) which connects directly to an American international operator for making collect and charge-account calls. To dial direct to the U.S. from Mexico, dial 95 + area code + number; from Spain dial 07 (wait for tone) + 1 + area code + number. Consult available charts or telephone personnel for direct dial calls to other countries.

Special Assistance

Personal assistance in making a call is usually available at the telephone office. Often a central desk is run by several operators who are willing to assist you. They will usually ask you to fill out a form with the country and the number you wish to call. A long-distance call is **una llamada a larga distancia** and an international call is **una llamada internacional**. A collect call is **una llamada a cobro revertido.**

* In Mexico, the phone is answered with the word **bueno.**

11 Reservations

¿———?
Smith?

¿—— ——. ——————?
Are you American?

——, ——— ——————.
Yes, I'm American.

————, ————,
Goodbye, madam,

———— ——————.
until tomorrow.

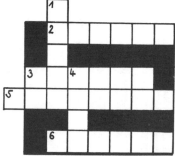

→
2 Hello (telephone)
3 Name
5 To reserve
6 Tomorrow

↓
1 Goodbye
4 Table

restourän'te	el restaurante	restaurant
kōmer'	comer	to eat
ke dese'•än kōmer'	¿qué desean comer?	What would you like to eat?
kär'ne	la carne	meat
peskä'dō	el pescado	fish
pō'lyō	el pollo	chicken
pō'lyō äsä'dō	pollo asado	roast chicken
tōrtē'lyä	la tortilla	omelet (Spain) bread-like tortilla (Mexico)
pä•e'lyä	la paella	paella (Spain)
sō'pä	la sopa	soup
sō'pä de ä'hō	sopa de ajo	garlic soup (Spain)
kre'mä de tōmä'te	crema de tomate	cream of tomato soup
tshē'le	el chile	mild or hot pepper (Mexico)
tshē'le relye'nō	chile relleno	stuffed pepper (Mexico)
än termēnä'dō	¿han terminado?	Have you finished?
koo•en'tä	la cuenta	bill

Meal times

Lunch is typically served between 1:00 PM and 3–4:00 PM. Dinner is served from approximately 8:00 PM and later. Many restaurants are closed at other hours. In-between-meal snacks (**tapas** or **pinchos**) are served at bars and cafés throughout the day.

Finding tables

Wait to be seated by the waiter in a restaurant or hotel dining room.

Tips

It is customary and considered polite to leave a tip to express satisfaction with a meal and service.

12 At the Restaurant

¿——— —————— —————?
What would you like to eat?

¿—————, ———————, ————— —————,
Meat, fish, roast chicken,

————————, ——————?
omelet, paella?

——— —————— ——————,
Two roast chickens,

——— —————.
please.

12 At the Restaurant

→
3 Meat
4 Rice dish
5 Soup

1 Omelet
2 Bill
4 Fish
6 Chicken

beber'	**beber**	*to drink*
ke kyer'en beber'	**¿qué quieren beber?**	*What would you like to drink?*
ä'gooä mēneräl'	**el agua mineral**	*mineral water*
kōnyäk'	**el coñac**	*brandy, cognac*
hoo'gō de närän'hä	**el jugo de naranja**	*orange juice*
vē'nō tēn'tō	**el vino tinto**	*red wine*
vē'nō bläng'kō	**el vino blanco**	*white wine*
tekē'lä	**la tequila**	*tequila*
serve'sä	**la cerveza**	*beer*
rōn'	**el ron**	*rum*
espänyōl'	**español**	*Spanish*
eskēsē'tō	**exquisito**	*exquisite*

Red Wine

Spain is famous for its excellent and flavorful red wines. The best-known wines come from the region of **La Rioja** in north-central Spain. Sherry (**jerez**), which comes from the city of Jerez in southern Spain, is made by adding cognac to the wine while it is fermenting.

Beer

Both Spain and Mexico produce delicious domestic beers. Several Mexican brands, such as **Corona, Dos Equis**, and **Tecate**, have become popular in the U.S.

Rum

Puerto Rico is known throughout the world for its fine rums. Be sure to try the dark and light varieties, as well as the different tropical rum drinks.

Sangría

Sangría is a sweet punch made of red wine, fruit, juices, and often brandy or other liquor. It is very refreshing when drunk cold on a hot day.

The bull in the picture is the logo for the brandy **Veterano**, made by the Osborne company in Spain.

13 Drinks

In Spain and Latin America, drinks are more expensive if you s[it]
down at a table, and cheaper if you stand at the bar.

___ _____,
A beer,
___ _____.
please.

__ ____ _____,
A red wine,
___ _____.
please.
__ ____ ____ _____
Spanish red wine
__ _____.
is exquisite.

→
1 Beer
4 Red (wine)
5 Juice

↓ 2 Wine
3 Water

ōˈlä	¡Hola!		Hello!
ke täl′	¿qué tal?		How's it going?
kōˈmō estäˈ ooste′	¿cómo está Ud.?		How are you?
kōˈmō se syen′te	¿cómo se siente?		How do you feel?
enferˈmō	enfermo		ill, sick
enferˈmä	enferma*		
estoi′ enferˈmō	estoy enfermo		I'm sick
kabeˈsä	la cabeza		head
me dooeˈle la kabeˈsä	me duele la cabeza		I have a headache
estōˈmägō	el estómago		stomach
dōlōr′	el dolor		pain
fyeˈbre	la fiebre		fever
ten′gō fyeˈbre	tengo fiebre		I have a fever
färmäˈsyä	la farmacia		pharmacy
pästēˈlyä	la pastilla		pill
äspērēˈnäs	las aspirinas		aspirin pills

The sign for a pharmacy in Spain:

---

* The word ends in -a if a woman is speaking and in -o of a man is speaking.

14 Sick

¡____!
Hello!

¡____, _____!
Hello, Carmen!

¿___ ___?
How's it going?

_____ _____.
I'm sick.

__ _____ __ _____.
I have a headache.

¿_____ ___ ___
Where is there a

_____?
pharmacy?

täk'sē	el taxi	taxi
pärä'dä de täk'sēs	la parada de taxis	taxi stand
lē'bre	libre	free (available)
lyä'me ooste' un täk'sē	llame Ud. un taxi	call a taxi
oon mōmen'tō	un momento	one moment
ädōn'de	¿adónde?	where to?
ä sän hoo•än'	a San Juan	to San Juan
äl ōtel' senträl'	al Hotel Central	to the Hotel Central
äl ä•erōpoo•er'tō	al aeropuerto	to the airport
ä lä cä'lye de lä kroos'	a la Calle de la Cruz	to Cruz (Cross) Street
ä lä ävenē'dä del mär	a la Avenida del Mar	to Mar (Sea) Avenue
äkē'	aquí	here
pä're ooste' äkē'	pare Ud. aquí	stop here
ve'ēnte mēl pesōs	veinte mil pesos	20,000 pesos

Taxi information

A taxi is available when the sign **LIBRE** or a green light is displayed.

Fares

For trips outside the city limits of larger cities, taxi drivers switch over to a different rate, which includes the trip back to the city. Always pay close attention to the price indicated on the taxi meter. In some countries, as in Spain, drivers are required to leave the meter on at all times. There may be an extra charge for large pieces of luggage.

If you notice a taxi without a meter (in the Canary Islands, for example), you should inquire about the appropriate fares (ask a hotel doorman or the taxi driver before getting in).

73

15 Taxi

3 Taxi stand

1 Stop (command)
2 Taxi
4 Here

Answers

Lesson 1

¿De dónde sale el vuelo dieciséis?
La puerta número dos.

Gracias.

Quiero facturar la maleta.
Muy bien.

Su tarjeta de embarque, señor.
Gracias.

Lesson 2

Tome su boleto

Gasolina super.
¿Cuánto?
Lleno, por favor.

Ceda el paso

Su boleto, por favor.
Mil pesos.

PUERTO VALLARTA, GUADALAJARA, MORELIA,
MEXICO, CUERNAVACA, PUEBLA, OAXACA

Lesson 3

Buenas tardes.
Buenas tardes, señor.

Una habitación, por favor.
Sí.
Una habitación doble.

¿Para cuántos días?
Para cinco días.

¿Cuánto cuesta la habitación?
Cinco mil pesetas.
Muy bien.
La tomo.

1 PRECIO	2 CINCO
2 DIA	4 BIEN
5 HABITACION	
6 SEÑOR	

Lesson 4

¿Dónde está el comedor?
A la derecha, señora.

Buenos días, señora.
¿Café o té?
Café con leche, por favor.

Aquí tiene Ud. el café,
el panecillo, la mermelada
y la mantequilla.

¿Desea Ud. jugo de naranja?
Sí.

2 MANTEQUILLA   1 LECHE
4 PANECILLO   3 TE
5 MERMELADA

Lesson 5

Una guía de Madrid,
por favor.
Muchas gracias.
De nada.

¿Dónde está
el Museo del Prado?
En el Paseo del Prado.

Tome Ud. el autobús.

¿Va este autobús
al Museo del Prado?
Sí.

¿Dónde está
el Museo del Prado?
No sé.

A la derecha.
Gracias, señor.

Una entrada, por favor.

1 TOME	2 MUSEO
5 MADRID	3 PRADO
6 ENTRADA	4 GUIA
8 AUTOBUS	7 TURISMO

Lesson 6

Un café solo, por favor.

¡Qué calor hace!

¿Es Ud. norteamericano?
Sí, soy de Nueva York.

Estados Unidos es bonito.
¡España también!

Me encanta España.
El vino, el sol . . .

¿Un cigarrillo?
Muchas gracias, señor.

Lesson 7

¿Cuánto cuestan
los anteojos de sol?
Cinco mil pesos.

Los tomo.

¿Algo más?
No, gracias.

¿Dónde hay
una oficina de cambio?
¿Una oficina de cambio?
Hay un banco ahí.

Buenos días, señor.
Quiero cambiar
doscientos dólares.

Son cuatrocientos mil pesos.

Gracias. Adiós.

2 PESETA   1 BANCO
3 CUANTO
4 CAMBIO

Lesson 8

Estas postales, por favor.
Trescientos pesos.

¿Tiene Ud. timbres?
No, señora,
la oficina de Correos
está ahí.

¿Cuánto cuesta una postal
para Estados Unidos?
Cien pesos.

81

Cinco timbres
de cien pesos,
por favor.

1 POSTAL
2 SELLOS
3 CORREOS
4 DOSCIENTOS

Lesson 9

Un helado, por favor.
¿Vainilla?
¿Chocolate?
¿Fresa?

Vainilla, por favor.

Un patín.
¿Cuánto cuesta
por hora?
Dos mil pesos.

Es muy caro.

Quiero una sombrilla.
¿Cuánto cuesta?
Diez mil pesos.

La tomo.

¿Algo más?
Aceite bronceador.

3 HELADO	1 CHOCOLATE
5 ACEITE	2 VAINILLA
7 SOMBRILLA	4 FRESA
8 HORA	6 CARO

Lesson 10

¿Qué quiere Ud.?
Cinco naranjas.

¿Algo más?
Un kilo de tomates, por favor.

Los plátanos están
muy buenos.
No, gracias.

Mire Ud. los ajos.
¡No, no!

¡Sí!
Una cabeza de ajos.
El ajo es muy bueno para ensalada de tomates.

1 PLATANO
2 AJO
3 NARANJA
4 TOMATE

Lesson 11

Dígame . . .

Quiero reservar
una mesa
para dos personas
para mañana por la noche.

Muy bien.
¿Su nombre, por favor?

Mi nombre es Smith.

83

¿Smith?
¿Es Ud. norteamericana?

Sí, soy nortemericana.

Adiós, señora,
hasta mañana.

2 DIGAME	1 ADIOS
3 NOMBRE	4 MESA
5 RESERVAR	
6 MAÑANA	

Lesson 12

Buenas tardes.
Una mesa para dos personas.

¿Qué desean comer?
¿Carne, pescado, pollo asado,
tortilla, paella?

Dos pollos asados, por favor.

¿Sopa?
¿Sopa de ajo?
¿Crema de tomate?

Dos cremas de tomate,
por favor.

Dos pollos asados.

¿Han terminado?
Sí.
La cuenta, por favor.

3 CARNE	1 TORTILLA
4 PAELLA	2 CUENTA
5 SOPA	4 PESCADO
	6 POLLO

84

Lesson 13

¿Qué quieren beber?
Un agua mineral.
Un coñac.
Un jugo de naranja.

Una cerveza, por favor.
Un vino tinto, por favor.
El vino tinto español
es exquisito.

1 CERVEZA	2 VINO
4 TINTO	3 AGUA
5 JUGO	

Lesson 14

¡Hola!
¡Hola, Carmen!

¿Qué tal?
Estoy enferma.
Me duele la cabeza.

¿Dónde hay una farmacia?

Me duele la cabeza.

Me duele el estómago.

Tengo fiebre.

Quiero aspirinas.

3	FARMACIA	1	ENFERMO
5	ESTOMAGO	2	PASTILLA
6	FIEBRE	4	CABEZA
7	DOLOR		

Lesson 15

Llame Ud. un taxi, por favor.
Sí, señor, un momento.

¿Adónde?
Al aeropuerto, por favor.

Pare Ud. aquí.

¿Cuánto cuesta?
Veinte mil pesos.

3	PARADA	1	PARE
		2	TAXI
		4	AQUI

Food & Drink

Puzzle on page 89

TE
AJO
VINO
CAFE
SOPA
CARNE
LECHE
POLLO
PAELLA
HELADO
TOMATE
CERVEZA
NARANJA
PESCADO
PLATANO
TORTILLA
MERMELADA
PANECILLO
MANTEQUILLA

Syllable Puzzle

Puzzle on page 106

1. AU TO BUS
2. BOL SA
3. CA BE ZA
4. CER VE ZA
5. EN TRA DA
6. FRE SA
7. GA SO LI NA
8. HE LA DO
9. ME SA
10. MIL
11. NA RAN JA
12. PES CA DO
13. PE SE TA
14. PLA TA NO
15. POS TAL
16. SOL
17. TA XI
18. TO MA TE
19. VI NO

Word-Building Puzzle

Puzzle on page 108

Spanish Islands: **ISLAS CANARIAS**

VINO
SELL**O**
CAB**E**Z**A**
PE**S**CADO
NARAN**JA**
SOMBRILLA
MES**A**

Spanish Novel:
DON QUIJOTE DE LA MANCHA

DOSCIENTOS
QUINCE
AJO
TOMA**TE**
DIEZ
GA**S**OLINA
ME**S**A
NARAN**JA**
CHO**C**OLATE

Spanish name of the Discoverer of America:
CRISTOBAL COLON

CE**R**VE**ZA**
VINO
PE**S**E**TA**
SO**L**
BARCE**LO**N**A**
CAFE
POLLO
CIN**C**O

88

Food & Drink

(Answers on page 87)

19 Spanish words related to food and drink appear in the diagram. They can be found horizontally or vertically. The 19 words are:

```
M E R M E L A D A P N
C A R N E I M I T E A
E L A H E L A D O S R
R O S T I P N O R C A
V I N O N A T N T A N
E P P M O N E S I D J
Z A L A T E Q U L O A
A E A T O C U D L O R
O L T E S I I C A F E
I L A F O L L E C H E
B A N Z I L L A A J O
S P O L L O A S O P A
```

V I N O

P A E L L A

Mini-Dictionary for Tourists

English-Spanish

Find the appropriate Spanish word as needed:

a/an	un, una	*bad*	malo	**B**
accident	accidente, choque	*bag*	bolsa	
		baggage check	consigna	
address	dirección	*bakery*	panadería	
admission ticket	entrada	*balcony*	balcón	
afternoon	tarde	*banana*	plátano	
air mattress	colchón neumático	*bank*	banco	
		bar	bar	
airplane	avión	*basement*	planta baja	
airport	aeropuerto	*bath*	baño	
all	todo	*bath towel*	toalla de baño	
ambulance	ambulancia	*bathing suit*	traje de baño	
American	norte ameri-cano	*battery*	pila	
		beach	playa	
and	y	*beach um-brella*	sombrilla	
anis	anís	*beans*	frijoles (Mex.)	
appetizers	entremeses	*beans (green)*	judías	
apple	manzana	*bed*	cama	
apple juice	jugo de man-zana	*beer*	cerveza	
		belt	cinturón	
arrival	llegada	*beverages*	bebidas	
artichoke	alcachofa	*bicycle*	bicicleta	
ashtray	cenicero	*big*	grande	
asparagus	espárragos	*bill*	cuenta	
attention	atención	*black*	negro	
avenue	avenida	*blanket*	cubierta, manta	
avocado	aguacate			

Mexican Recipe

Guacamole	*Avocado Dip*
1/2 onion, chopped *2 hot peppers, chopped* *1-2 sprigs coriander* *Salt to taste*	Blend these ingredients into a smooth paste.
2 avocados, peeled and * pit removed*	Scoop out meat, mash and blend into above mixture.
1 tomato, chopped, *Dash of lemon juice*	Stir into mixture, serve immediately.

Guacamole is best served immediately, with corn tortilla chips or raw vegetables.

blouse	blusa	castle	castillo, alcázar
blue	azul	cat	gato
board (food)	pensión	cathedral	catedral
boarding pass	tarjeta de embarque	cave	cueva
boat	barco	centimeter	centímetro
border	frontera	certain	seguro
bottle	botella	champagne	champán, cava
bread	pan	cheap	barato
breakdown	avería	check	cheque
breakfast	desayuno	(verb)	facturar
brakes	frenos	cheese	queso
bridge	puente	cherry	cereza
broken	roto	chicken	pollo
brown	marrón	chick-peas	garbanzos
building	edificio	chocolate	chocolate
bull	toro	chop (of meat)	chuleta
bullfight	corrida	church	iglesia
bull ring	plaza de toros	cigar	puro, cigarro
bus	autobús	cigarette	cigarrillo
bus stop	parada	cinnamon	canela
business district	centro comercial	city	ciudad
		clams	almejas
butcher shop	carnicería	clock	reloj
butter	mantequilla	closed	cerrado
buy	comprar	clothing	ropa
		cloud	nube
		cloudy	nuboso
		clutch	embrague
cake	pastel	coast	costa
call	llamar	coffee	café
camera	cámara	(black)	sólo
camping	camping	(with milk)	con leche
can opener	abrelatas	coin	moneda
Canadian	canadiense	cold	frío
candy	caramelos	collision	choque
car	coche	color	color
car rental	alquiler de coches	comb	peine
		construction	obras
carrot	zanahoria	consulate	consulado
cashier	caja	cookies	galletas

93

Spanish Recipe

Paella valenciana   *Valencian Paella*

1/3 cup (2-1/2 fluid ounces) olive oil	Heat oil in deep pan.
2 cloves of garlic, minced	Add vegetables and the chicken.
1 tomato, chopped	
1/2 green pepper, chopped	Season with salt and cook until chicken is done and vegetables sautéed.
2 chicken breasts, skinned & deboned, chopped	
4 small chicken thighs	
Salt to taste	

2 cups (170 g) short grain rice	Add to chicken, bring to a boil, cover, and simmer,
Pinch of ground saffron	stirring occasionally until
5 cups (1.2 L) water	rice is tender.

8–12 jumbo shrimp, peeled and cooked	Add shrimp, mussels, and lemon juice and cook
8–12 mussels, cooked	until shellfish is heated
Juice of 1/2 lemon	through.
	Serve immediately.

Variations: Additional ingredients, such as peas and squid or other seafood, may be added.

cool	fresco	*downtown*	centro	
corkscrew	sacacorchos	*dress*	vestido	
corn	maíz	*drink*	beber, tomar	
cost (does it)	cuesta	*drink (cold)*	refresco	
country	país	*driver's license*	permiso de conducir	
cow	vaca			
cream	crema	*duck*	pato	
cream (filling)	nata			
credit card	tarjeta de crédito	*east*	este	**E**
crossroads	cruce	*eat*	comer	
cruise	crucero	*egg*	huevo	
cucumber	pepino	*eggplant*	berenjena	
cup	taza	*elevator*	ascensor	
customs	aduana	*embassy*	embajada	
		empty	vacío	
danger	peligro	*endive*	escarola	
date	fecha	*engine*	motor	
day	día	*entrance*	entrada	
dead (battery)	muerto descargado	*evening*	tarde	
decaffeinated	descafeinado	*exchange (verb)*	cambio, cambiar	
declare	declarar	*excursion*	excursión	
delay	retraso, demora	*excuse me*	perdón	
dentist	dentista	*exit*	salida	
departure	salida	*expensive*	caro	
dessert	postre	*express train*	tren expreso	
diarrhea	diarrea	*eyeglasses*	anteojos, gafas	
dining car	coche-restaurante			
dining room	comedor	*far*	lejos	**F**
dinner	cena	*fast*	rápido	
disco	discoteca	*fever*	fiebre	
dish	plato	*few*	pocos	
distance	distancia	*fig*	higo	
doctor	médico, doctor	*fillet*	filete, solomillo	
door	puerta	*film*	película	
double room	habitación doble	*filter*	filtro	
		fine (fee)	multa	
		fire	incendio	

Spanish Recipe

Tortilla española	*Spanish Omelet*
3 potatoes, thinly sliced *2 onions, finely chopped* *1 cup (8 fluid ounces)* *olive oil* *Salt and pepper*	Fry potatoes and onions in olive oil over medium heat until potatoes are soft and golden.
4 eggs *1/4 cup (2 fluid ounces)* *milk*	Beat eggs and milk in bowl. Remove potato mixture from skillet and blend into egg mixture. Pour thin layer of oil into pan and add egg mixture. When omelet begins to solidify, turn over to cook on other side.

Serve with a green salad.

Variation: You may wish to add chopped green peppers, diced tomatoes, or other diced vegetables to omelet.

(*extinguisher*)	extintor
fireman	bombero
first class	primera clase
fish	pescado
(*codfish*)	bacalao
(*hake*)	merluza
(*to fish*)	pescar
flamenco	flamenco
flash	flash
flight	vuelo
floor	piso
food	comida
for	para, por
fork	tenedor
free	libre
free (*price*)	gratis
french fries	papas fritas (Mex.) patatas fritas (Sp.)
fresh	fresco
Friday	viernes
fried	frito
fried eggs	huevos fritos
friend	amigo
fruit	fruta
full	lleno
game	juego
garage	garage
garbage	basura
garlic	ajo
gas station	estación de servicio, gasolinera
gasoline	gasolina
gate	puerta
gearshift	cambio de velocidades
glass	vaso, copa
good	bueno
good day	buenos días
good evening	buenas tardes
good morning	buenos días
good night	buenas noches
goodbye	adiós
gram	gramo
grape	uva
gray	gris
green	verde
green beans	judías verdes
groceries	comestibles
ground floor	planta baja
guide	guía
guided tour	visita con guía
gym	gimnasio

H

hair	pelo
hair salon	peluquería
half	medio
ham	jamón
(*sliced*)	jamón york
(*prosciutto*)	jamón serrano
hamburger	hamburguesa
handbag	bolsa
handkerchief	pañuelo
hat	sombrero
head	cabeza
heat	calor
hello	hola
(*telephone*)	dígame (Sp.) bueno (Mex.)
help	ayuda
Help!	¡Socorro!
hen	gallina
here	aquí
highway	carretera, autopista

Spanish-Mexican Recipe

Sangría

Sangria

---

3 parts ginger ale
1 part red wine
Brandy or Triple-sec
* to taste*
Sliced apples
Sliced oranges
Sliced lemon
[block of ice—optional]

Combine all ingredients
in a large punch bowl,
stir to mix. Refrigerate
and serve chilled. Pour
over block of ice to keep
cold.

Sangria is best served cold and complements any snack
or summer meal.

Variations: Other types of fruit may be added: peaches,
bananas, and pears. Different types of liquor (rum, for
example) may also be used.

holidays	(días) festivos	large	grande
honey	miel	lawyer	abogado
hospital	hospital	leave	salir
hostel	hostal	left (direction)	izquierda
hot	caliente	lemon	limón
hotel	hotel	less	menos
hour	hora	letter	carta
house	casa	lighter	encendedor, fuego
how	cómo		
how much	cuánto	liter	litro
hunt	cazar	little	pequeño
hurt	doler	liver	hígado
husband	esposo, marido	lobster	langosta
		local train	tren de cercanías
I	yo	loin	lomo
ice cream	helado	(cut of	
ice cube	cubito de hielo	meat)	
		long	largo
I.D. card	documento de identidad	long-distance train	tren de largo recorrido
ill	enfermo	look (at)	mirar
indigestion	indigestión	lose	perder
information	información	luggage	equipaje
insurance	seguros	luggage cart	portamaletas
international	internacional	lunch	almuerzo
international flight	vuelo internacional		
island	isla	madam, Mrs.	señora
		magazine	revista
jam	confitura	mail	correos
juice	jugo	mailbox	buzón
		man	hombre, señor, caballero
key	llave		
kidneys	riñones	map	mapa
kilo	kilo	(of city)	plano
kilometer	kilómetro	market	mercado
knife	cuchillo	marmelade	mermelada
		matador	matador
lamb	cordero	meal	comida
lane	carril		

M

Numbers

0	cero	30	treinta
1	uno	31	treinta y uno
2	dos	32	treinta y dos
3	tres	33	treinta y tres . . .
4	cuatro		
5	cinco	40	cuarenta
6	seis	41	cuarenta y uno . . .
7	siete		
8	ocho	50	cincuenta
9	nueve	60	sesenta
		70	setenta
10	diez	80	ochenta
11	once	90	noventa
12	doce		
13	trece	100	cien
14	catorce	103	ciento tres
15	quince	150	ciento cincuenta
16	dieciséis	200	doscientos
17	diecisiete	500	quinientos
18	dieciocho	700	setecientos
19	diecinueve	900	novecientos
20	veinte	1,000	mil
21	veintiuno	3,000	tres mil
22	veintidós	5,000	cinco mil
23	veintitrés	1,000,000	un millón

meat	carne	*north*	norte
melon	melón	*not*	no
(*water—*)	sandía	*nothing*	nada
menu	menú	*number*	número
meter	metro		
Mexican	mexicano	*occupied*	ocupado **O**
milk	leche	*oil*	aceite
mineral water	agua mineral	*oil change*	cambio de
minute	minuto		aceite
Miss	señorita	*oil level*	nivel de aceite
mist	niebla	*olives*	aceitunas
Mr.	señor	*omelet*	tortilla
Mrs.	señora	*onion*	cebolla
moment	momento	*only*	sólo
monastery	monasterio	*open*	abierto
money	dinero	*opener*	
Monday	lunes	(*bottles*)	abridor
moped	moto	(*cans*)	abrelatas
more	más	*orange*	naranja
morning	mañana	*orange juice*	jugo de
mosque	mezquita		naranja
motor	motor		
mushrooms	champiñones,	*packet*	paquete **P**
	setas	*paddleboat*	patín
mussels	mejillones	*pain*	dolor
mustard	mostaza	*painting*	cuadro
my	mi	*pair*	par
		palace	palacio
		pamphlet	folleto
		pants	pantalones
name	nombre	*parking*	estaciona-
(*last name*)	apellido		miento
napkin	servilleta	*party*	fiesta
national	nacional	*passenger*	pasajero
nationality	nacionalidad	*passport*	pasaporte
necktie	corbata	*patio*	patio
newspaper	periódico	*pay*	pagar
nice	amable	*peach*	melocotón
no	no	*peas*	guisantes
noodles	fideos, pastas	*pedestrian*	peatón
noon	mediodía	*pedestrian*	zona peatonal
normal	normal	*zone*	

pen (*ballpoint*)	bolígrafo	raisins	uvas pasas
peninsula	península	range (*of mountains*)	sierra
pepper (*spice*)	pimienta		
(*vegetable*)	pimiento	razor	máquina de afeitar
pepperoni	chorizo		
person	persona	reception	recepción
photograph	foto	recipe	receta
pill	pastilla	red	rojo
pineapple	piña	(*wine*)	tinto
place	lugar	Red Cross	Cruz Roja
place setting	cubierto	refrigerator	refrigerador, frigorífico (Sp.)
platform	andén		
pleasant	agradable		
please	por favor		
police	policía	rent (*verb*)	alquilar
pool	piscina	rental car	coche de alquiler
pork	cerdo		
port (*city*)	puerto	rest room	servicios
post office	oficina de correos	restaurant	restaurante
		rice	arroz
postcard	postal	right (*direction*)	derecha
potato	papa (Mex.)		
potato chips	patata (Sp.)	river	río
	papas fritas	roast chicken	pollo asado
poultry	aves	robbery	robo
price	precio	rock	roca, piedra
price list	lista de precios	roll (*dinner*)	panecillo
		room	habitación, cuarto (Mex.)
prohibited	prohibido		
public	público	round trip ticket	billete de ida y vuelta
pull	tirar		
push	empujar	route	itinerario, ruta
Q question	pregunta		
quick	rápido	row	fila
		salad	ensalada
rabbit	conejo	sale	oferta, rebaja
R railroad	ferrocarril		
rain	lluvia	salt	sal
(*to rain*)	llover	sandwich	sandwich
rainy	lluvioso	sanitary napkin	compresa

sardine	sardina	soup	sopa
Saturday	sábado	south	sur
sauce	salsa	Spain	España
sausage	salchicha	Spaniard	español
schedule	horario	Spanish	español
screwdriver	destornillador	spare part	pieza de recambio
sea	mar		
seafood store	pescadería	spare tire	rueda de repuesto
see	ver	specialty of the day	menú del día
seatbelt	cinturón de seguridad	spinach	espinacas
serious	grave	spoon	cuchara
shampoo	champú	sports	deportes
sherry	jerez	square (of town)	plaza
ship	barco, buque		
shirt	camisa	squid	calamares
shoes	zapatos	stairs	escalera
short circuit	cortocircuito	stamp	timbre (Mex.)
shower	ducha		sello (Sp.)
shower (rain)	chubasco	station	estación
shrimp	camarones (Mex.)	statue	estatua
	gambas (Sp.)	steak	bistec
		steal	robar
sick	enfermo	steering wheel	volante
signature	firma		
single room	habitación individual	stew	cocido
		steward	camarero
sir, Mr.	señor	stewardess	azafata
size	taller, tamaño	stockings (pantyhose)	medias panty
skirt	falda		
sleeper car (2nd class)	coche-cama, coche-litera	stomach	estómago
		stop	parar
slides	diapositivas	(bus stop)	parada
small	pequeño	store	tienda
smoke	fumar	storm	tempestad
snails	caracoles	straight ahead	todo derecho
snow	nieve		
(to snow)	nevar	strawberry	fresa
soap	jabón	street	calle
socks	calcetines	subway	metro

103

sugar	azúcar	this	este, esta
suitcase	maleta	Thursday	jueves
sun	sol	ticket	boleto
Sunday	domingo		billete (Sp.)
sunglasses	anteojos/gafas de sol	(travel)	pasaje
suntan lotion	crema solar	(admission)	entrada
suntan oil	aceite bronceador	(—counter)	taquilla
supermarket	supermercado	time	hora
supper	cena	tip	propina
supplement	suplemento	tissues	pañuelos de papel
sure	seguro	to	a
sweater	suéter	today	hoy
sweet	dulce	toilet	servicios
swim	nadar	toll	peaje
		tomato	tomate
		tomorrow	mañana
T table	mesa	toothbrush	cepillo de dientes
tablet (pill)	pastilla	tour	visita
take	tomar	tourist	turista
taxi	taxi	tourist office	oficina de turismo
taxi stand	parada de taxi		
tea	té	towel	toalla
telegram	telegrama	town hall	ayuntamiento
telephone	teléfono	towtruck	servicio de grúa
(—book)	guía de teléfonos		
(—booth)	cabina telefónica	traffic	tráfico
		traffic light	semáforo
(—number)	número de teléfono	train	tren
		travel agency	agencia de viajes
temperature	temperatura		
		trip	viaje
tennis	tenis	Tuesday	martes
tennis court	pista de tenis	tuna	atún
terrace	terraza		
thank you	gracias		
theater	teatro	umbrella	paraguas
there	ahí	U.S.	Estados Unidos
there is	hay		
thermostat	termostato	unleaded	sin plomo

valley	valle	wet	mojado
vanilla	vainilla	wheel	rueda
veal	ternera	when	cuándo
vegetables	legumbres	where	dónde
(green—)	verduras	where to	adónde
very	muy	which	qué, cuál
view	vista	white	blanco
vinegar	vinagre	who	quién
		why	por qué
		wide	ancho
waiter	camarero	wife	esposa,
waitress	camarera		mujer
walk	paseo	wind	viento
(to walk)	pasear,	windshield	parabrisas
	dar un	windshield	limpia-
	paseo	wipers	parabrisas
want	querer	wine	vino
ware	mercancía	(red—)	vino tinto
warm	caliente,	(rosé—)	vino rosado
	cálido	(white—)	vino blanco
warning	señal de	winecellar	bodega
	peligro	with	con
wash	lavar	without	sin
water	agua	witness	testigo
(drinkable—)	agua potable	woman	mujer, dama
water ski	esquí	workshop	taller
	náutico	wounded	herido
watermelon	sandía		
WC	WC, servicios	year	año
wear (verb)	llevar	yellow	amarillo
weather	tiempo	yes	sí
Wednesday	miércoles	yesterday	ayer
week	semana	yield	ceda el paso
weigh	pesar	you	usted (Ud.)
weight	peso	your	su
welcome	bienvenido		
well	bien	zoo	parque
west	oeste		zoológico

Y

Z

105

Syllable Puzzle

(Answers on page 87)

Form 19 words from these syllables and write them down. Picture clues and the number of syllables in each word are given on the next page.

AU	BE	BOL	BUS	CA	CA	CER	DA
DO	DO	EN	FRE	GA	HE	JA	LA
LI	MA					ME	MIL
NA	NA					NO	NO
PE	PES					PLA	POS
RAN	SA					SA	SA
SE	SO	SOL	TA	TA	TA	TAL	TE
TO	TO	TRA	VE	VI	XI	ZA	ZA

107

Word-Building Puzzle

(Answers on page 88)

Write the letters of the Spanish words in the boxes as indicated. For example, if the number "2" appears, write the second letter of the word suggested by the picture.

Spanish Islands:

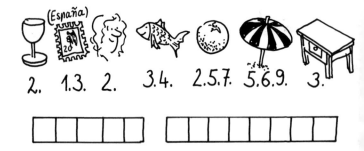

2.   1.3.   2.   3.4.   2.5.7.   5.6.9.   3.

Spanish Novel:

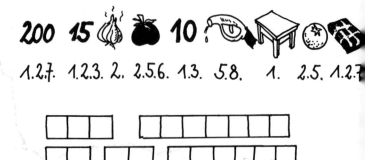

1.2.7.   1.2.3.   2.   2.5.6.   1.3.   5.8.   1.   2.5.   1.2.7.

Spanish Name of the Discoverer of America:

1.3.   2.   3.5.   2.   1.2.6.   1.   2.3.5.   3.

Important Addresses

In Mexico:

U.S. Embassy
(Embajada de los Estados Unidos):
Paseo de la Reforma 305, 06500 México D.F.

Canadian Embassy
(Embajada de Canadá):
Schiller 529, 11560 México, D.F.

British Embassy
(Embajada de Gran Bretaña):
Lerma 71, Apto. 96 bis, 06500 México, D.F.

Australian Embassy
(Embajada de Australia):
Plaza Polanco Torre B, Jaime Balmes 11, 10$^{\underline{o}}$, 11510 México, D.F

U.S. Consulates (consulados):
Ciudad Juarez: Avenida López Mateos 924N; Guadalajara: Progreso 175; Monterrey: Avenida Constitución 411 Poniente 64000 Tijuana: Tapachula 96; Hermosillo: Monterrey 141; Matamoros Avenida Primera No. 2002; Mazatlán: 6 Circunvalación 126, Centro; Mérida: Paseo Montejo 453; Nuevo Laredo: Calle Allend 3330.

In Spain:

U.S. Embassy
(Embajada de los Estados Unidos):
Serrano 75, 28006 Madrid

Candadian Embassy
(Embajada de Canadá):
Núñez de Balboa 35, Edificio Goya, 28001 Madrid

British Embassy
(Embajada de Gran Bretaña):
Fernando el Santo 16, 28010 Madrid

Australian Embassy
(Embajada de Australia):
Paseo de la Castellana 143, 2^{O}, Edificio Cuzco 1, 28046 Madrid

U.S. Consulates (consulados):
Barcelona: Vía Layetana 33; Bilbao: Avenida del Ejército 11-3, 48014 Bilbao